The Toy Farm

Story by Jenny Giles
Illustrations by Priscilla Cutter

One day at school, Sarah and Kiran
made a toy farm.
First, they made
a little farmhouse.

Then they made fences out of cardboard
for all the toy animals.

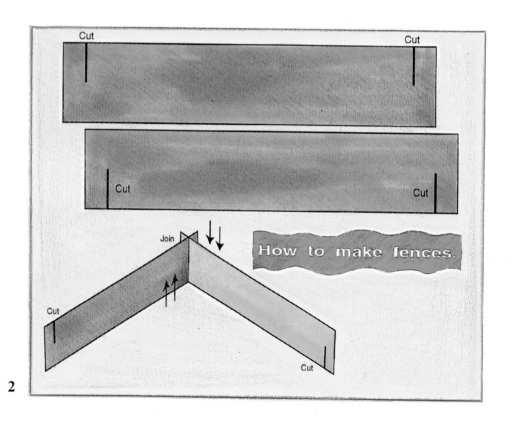

How to make fences.

"That's a very good farm,"
said Mrs. Webb.
"It can stay here
where we can all see it."

"Look at our forest," said Thomas.

"I made the small trees," said Jamie,
"and Thomas made the tall ones."

How to make trees.

At recess,
Thomas and Jamie played soccer outside.
Thomas kicked the ball to Jamie,
but it went over Jamie's head
and into the classroom.

"Oh, no!" cried Jamie.
"The girls' farm is broken."

"Come on!" said Thomas.
"We will have to fix it
  before they see it!"

"I have fixed the house,"
  said Thomas,
"but do the sheep go here?"

"No," said Jamie,
"and the fences don't look right.
  What can we do?"

"We can put some of our trees
on the farm," said Thomas.
"Then it will look better!"

"Yes!" said Jamie.
"The farm needs some trees."

Then Sarah and Kiran
came back inside.
"Who moved all our fences
and animals?" cried Sarah.

"And who put these **trees** here?"
asked Kiran.

Sarah looked at Jamie and Thomas.
Kiran looked at the ball
down on the floor.

"We broke your farm," said Thomas,
"but we didn't mean to."

"We are very sorry," said Jamie.
"We tried to fix it."

"We put some of our trees
on it for you," said Thomas.

"Well…" said Sarah, slowly.
"I do like the trees."

"Yes," said Kiran. "So do I,
and animals like to be under trees
when it's hot."

"Right!" said Thomas.
"You can have **all** our trees."

So Sarah and Kiran
and the boys
fixed the farm together.

"Look at our farm now, Mrs. Webb,"
called Sarah.

"It's got trees for all the animals,"
said Jamie.

"That's the best farm
I have ever seen!"
said Mrs. Webb.